"Murguía with a tango unleashed, a city on fire, a rendez-vous of homage, manifesto, revenge and transcendence—he is alone, without a face, yet recognizable in every body that swims through the under-streets of the City, of Paris, of Havana, of bombed-out-Here's-and-There's and the stripped down body of all of us. No stones are left unturned; hypnotic, alarming, "melodramático," rough-lovin', unkempt, "dangerous," and ready to battle at the center of the scorched core. "I didn't cheat," one poem admits. He is on trial—fire-spitter and disassembler of cultural falsifications, in "strange" and romantic moods, the poems scatter truth and aim and blow and burn and rise unto the flagless sky— ". . . a country of oceans and mountains." Murguía gets there. Alone, because few embark on that voyage. An astonishing, brutal nakedness. Love, that is. No book like it. An unimaginable heart of and for the people —a ground-breaking prize."

—Juan Felipe Herrera, Poet Laureate of California

"In the city of poets, Murguía has become the activist voice of refugees and exiles—as so many of us are, even as natives—at the center of the Americas. Disguised by its sensuous intimacy, soothing and ennobling, his is a poetry that arms the resistance."

—Dagoberto Gilb, author of *The Magic of Blood*

STRAY POEMS

STRAY POEMS

Alejandro Murguía

Para Luis Rodriguez
en solidaridad
Alejandro
murguía

Poet Laureate Series Number 6

Nov 21
2015

City Lights Foundation
San Francisco

Cover photo: Luis Delgado
Cover design: emdash

Note: Poems that appear bilingually were originally written in
Spanish. All the English translations are by the author.

Library of Congress Cataloging-in-Publication Data
Murguía, Alejandro, 1949–
 [Poems. Selections]
 Stray poems / Alejandro Murguía.
     pages cm. — (San Francisco poet laureate series ; no. 6)
 I. Title.
 PS3563.U7255A6 2014
 811'.54—dc23
                            2013040667

CITY LIGHTS FOUNDATION publications are published at the City
Lights Bookstore, 261 Columbus Avenue, San Francisco, CA 94133.
www.citylights.com

These poems are for the community
of the Mission District,
La Misión, San Pancho, mi gente, mi pueblo.

CONTENTS

INAUGURAL ADDRESS

Thank you all very much for attending this event that honors not just poets, poetry, but also the entire poetic/literary community of San Francisco.

We are so lucky to be able to gather to celebrate with poetry, when so much of the world is covered in violence, prejudice, hatred, intolerance, war and bigotry. We are truly blessed to live in a city like San Francisco, a city of poets.

I am truly honored to be with you here today.

Let me tell you a story: I was born in California but raised in Mexico City and Tijuana since I was about one year old to about six years old. The first time I recited poetry I was five years old in the first grade in Tijuana. I was on a balcony overlooking the entire student body in the school yard. It was a poem about Columbus—"Las Tres Carabelas." Ironic, I know.

Then when we return to the U.S., California, I arrive like any other immigrant. I don't know a single word of English. I don't know a thing about the culture. I am lost. I lose language. I am silent for a long time. I still vividly remember the very first words I ever spoke in English: "Pepsi, please."

Let me say—It has been a long road from that five-year-old on that schoolyard balcony to this stage. In particular I want to thank Magaly y Marisol for their patience.

I'm under no illusion that this laureateship is an individual honor—I know better than anyone that this is a recognition that belongs to my community, that it is about the contributions of the Latino community and the Mission community to the vibrant literary scene that is San Francisco.

I also know that there are other more deserving poets who would have stood here long before I ever would have, had it not been for the quirks of fate. Serafin Syquia, Buriel Clay II, Al Robles, and also those who in the future would have been poet laureate had the calavera catrina not taken them out to dance, Victor Martínez, and Piri Thomas, whose words I recall every day: "Every poet a child and every child a poet."

But also others such as Víctor Hernández Cruz, Ntozake Shange and Jessica Hagedorn, writers who I grew up with and worked with. But in particular, one poet who should be standing here is Roberto Vargas, had revolution, politics and life not gotten in the way.

These are the poets I grew up with, reading in cafés and bars—like the Coffee Gallery when Carolee Sanchez was running it, and at the Ribeltad Vorden, where I met John Ross, Kell Robertson, Wayne Miller and George Tsongas.

I cut my teeth reading in workingmen's bars, where if you didn't hold their attention they might boo you off the stage, tell you to go home. I always say that the first time I was paid for a reading it was two beers. Actually, it was only one beer because the other one was thrown at me.

When Mayor Lee called to ask if I would accept being Poet Laureate, I answered, "Only in the name of my community." Then my next thought was, *Does this honor come with a parking permit?* You have no idea how many poems I've written on the back of parking tickets. Have you ever tried a haiku for a parking ticket?

That's where that stipend is going for that you've heard so much chisme about.

So when I talk about community I mean all of us—what we have in common, in communion—what we hold together. And part of what we have in common is the literary history of San Francisco.

San Francisco has many parallel literary histories. One of these histories, the one I trace for myself, is a history that has often been lost and at the same time preserved—for example, the history of the Ramaytush, the first-nation people who lived along the creeks that flowed through what is now the Mission District: Mission, Precita, Islais, Serpentine; and the first chants, the first songs heard here, and hence, the first poetry: Ishman colma, carac yonabi acho isha hacheche asmush harwec irshah—sun, moon , sky, village, friend, alive, we eat, drink, sing and dance.

Or the diaries of discovery written by the first westerners, men like Pedro Font—a priest in Portola's expedition who was the first to describe the Farallons and also a point near present-day Point Reyes, named Punto Murguía, and whether poetic or not, these writings are still part of this other history. And what about the Chileans who shipped here from the Southern Hemisphere in the 1840s bringing the old mining songs and settling in communities like what is now North Beach? The songs and yearnings of Latin America, transposed and fused to this landscape. Pablo Neruda, for example, writing his play "Fulgor y Muerte de Joaquín Murieta," "Splendor and Death of Joaquín Murieta" about a legendary figure of California.

So Latin America fused to the history of San Francisco, and vice versa—San Francisco fused to the memory of Latin America.

One of the first poems I wrote in San Francisco was one afternoon in the mini-park there on Capp Street and 19th. I'm going to reach way into the archive for this one. It is written in the language of the barrio, known as Caló, and I'm going to read it how it was written, porque, porque—me da la chingada gana.

O California

Se fueron por el Camino Real
Ese largo y triste camino de eucaliptos
Cargados con frijol y maíz
Y llegaron en lowered-down Chevy ranflas
Con gafas fileros y tomando botellas de tequila
Que decían Made in Mexico
Hablando tres palabras de inglés
Apple pie y coffee
Y cantando—Vámonos a California
Vámonos a California

Se iban por el alambre
Indios de calzón blanco y huarache
Y aterrizaban
Pochos, pachucos, perdidos
Vatos locos con tatuajes mágicos de vida y muerte
Esperando en las esquinas el Big Hit
The 5-10 of Caliente race track
That never came

Cabuleando—esta sí es la vida gacha cucaracha
Y cantando
Vámonos a California, vámonos a California

They came from New York, New York
The Big Apple to the Big Orange
Yorubas, jíbaros, borinqueños
Piel color café oscuro
Ojos de verde cocodrilo
Y un ka-ta-tún-tún-tún
De viejas selvas ancestrales
But now with a pocket full of cancelled tickets
To the promised land
They were singing
Vámonos
Vámonos
Vámonos a California!

JOSÉ CORONEL URTECHO—THE PRECURSOR

Although San Francisco, and in particular, the Mission District, has served as a greenhouse for many Central American writers during their periods of exile, most notably during the decades from the 1970s to the present, Central American writers have lived in and written about San Francisco since the 1920s when José Coronel Urtecho penned his essay "Mis 'Gay Twenties,'" published in his book *Rápido Tránsito al Ritmo de Norteamérica.*

In this autobiographical essay, José Coronel Urtecho describes the life of a young Nicaraguan living with his family on Van Ness Avenue, near Vallejo Street, and attending Commerce High School to learn English. In many ways, Urtecho's essay is the precursor of Central American writing in the Bay Area: he touches on themes that will occupy future generations—the rapid pace of the big city; the glamour of its nightlife; alienation, racism, solitude. He also grafts English words and phrases to his Spanish to more fully capture his experience as a Central American in the United States, always indicating with italics that the English words are foreign. I will quote part of one sentence to illustrate my point: "A la hora del *lunch*, la quieta calle frente a la escuela cerrábase para el tráfico de vehículos y se llenaba, sobre todo, de muchachas que *lonchaban* en las cafeterías. . . ." (page 30).

On his return to Nicaragua, his suitcase stuffed with the poems of Walt Whitman, Ezra Pound, Carl Sandburg, Edna St. Vincent Millay and other Modernist poets, this influence would revolutionize the poetry of his native land. From this cultural poetic interchange, emanating in part from San Francisco, the most important literary movement of Central America in the 20th century emerged, the Vanguard Movement of Nicaragua, which influenced world-renowned poets as diverse as Pablo Antonio Cuadra and Ernesto Cardenal, the greatest living poet of Latin America at this time.

We also cannot deny or underestimate the influence of Central American poetry here in San Francisco, in particular, the poetry of Claribel Alegría, Daisy Zamora, Gioconda Belli, Otto René Castillo and Ernesto Cardenal and the great influence of Roque Dalton, whose life and work inspired in the early 1980s the formation and translations undertaken by the Roque Dalton Cultural Brigade, such as *Volcán*, *Poemas Clandestinos*, and *Tomorrow Triumphant: Selected Poems of Otto René Castillo*. The work of this cultural brigade was instrumental in forming a new consciousness among poets as well as encouraging more translations from Latin America. Even today Roque Dalton's work has touched most every poet I know here in San Francisco and most recently had a direct or indirect influence on the Revolutionary Poets Brigade.

I believe the collective work of the Roque Dalton Cultural Brigade set a standard that will last a long time. It is also the duty of the poet to recover the lost texts of our continent, the forgotten writers, and reread them and preserve their work for future generations. It is important, too, to read widely from many different streams of poetry, even bad poetry, so that you learn what good poetry sounds like.

In the late 1960s and early 1970s and up to the present, the contributions of Latino poetic voices to the history and poetic-literary movements of San Francisco play a prominent role. One of those was Dr. Fernando Alegría, a professor at Stanford and cultural ambassador for the Salvador Allende government, who did so much to link Latin America to San Francisco. In particular, he organized one of the most momentous readings ever—the reading for Pablo Neruda and Salvador Allende on October 4, 1973, at Glide Memorial Church, attended by some of the great poets of our time, including Diane di Prima, Víctor Hernández Cruz, Lawrence Ferlinghetti, Janice Mirikitani, Jean Franco, Kathleen Frazer, David Henderson, Ishmael Reed, Nanos Valaoritis, Nina Serrano and Roberto Vargas, to name a few.

Latino poets have enriched and enhanced the poetry of San Francisco with their bilingual writings and readings, their publications, their political perspectives and their approach to poetry—to quote the Salvadoran poet Roque Dalton, the belief that "poetry, like bread, is for everyone."

At the same time the people of San Francisco, and in particular its poetic community and literary community, have been and continue to be a source of solidarity, without which this most recent flowering of Latino poetic voices could not have bloomed so brilliantly.

HISTORICAL OVERVIEW OF THE 1970S

In 1970 the first Latino poet to be published was Amilcar Lobos, of Guatemalan background. His collection of poems *Quetzal* was published by Casa Hispana de Bellas Artes, located at that time at 362 Capp Street.

But the most influential, both artistically and politically, of this wave of Central American poets, is the Nicaraguan Roberto Vargas (born 1941), who migrated to San Francisco in 1946. He grew up among the new generation of Nicaraguans coming to the Bay Area during and after World War II. As a young man, he traveled to the Far East as a merchant seaman, worked in a mattress factory, then became one of the few Latinos to participate in both the Beat-era North Beach scene and the Haight-Ashbury scene. With the rise of the Vietnam anti-war movement and the civil rights movement of the 1960s, Vargas becomes active in the Chicano movement and the Third World liberation movement. This activity—the Brown Berets and Los Siete de la Raza—inspires some of the best poetry of that era: "Canto al Tercer Marcha de Delano," "They Blamed It on Reds," and "Elegy Pa' Gringolandia." His influence is such that his work appears in all the major Chicano anthologies of that period, including *Aztlán: An Anthology on Mexican-American Literature*, edited by Luis Valdez and Stan Steiner (1971), and *Festival de Flor y Canto*, edited by Alurista et al., (University of Southern California Chicano Studies, 1974).

His first book of poems, *Primeros Cantos*, defines his style—rhythmic and imagistic. The poems are meant to be performed, which the poet often did accompanied by congeros. The images are clear, precise, and flowing, often without connecting phrases, just the pure image carrying the poem.

Vargas captures the breath of his experience in a prose-poem titled "Then There Was. . . ," a jazz-like riff recounting the poet's early years in this country, from his arrival through his high school years in the Mission District, his stint in the Marine Corps, and finally the death of his first wife. The influence of United States music, rhythm and blues, and oldies, mixed with boleros, mixed with nostalgia for his homeland and his emerging political consciousness, mark this prose-poem as one of the most innovative of his works. It was first published in *City Magazine* in 1975, and later in *Nicaragua, Yo Te Canto Besos Balas y Sueños de Libertad*, in 1980.

A defining moment in the poet's life occurs when an earthquake destroys Managua, Nicaragua, in December 1972. After this catastrophe, the Nicaraguan dictator Anastasio Somoza tightens his grip on the country. Vargas, besides being a key organizer of the *Gaceta Sandinista*, the official publication of the Frente Sandinista de Liberación Nacional, the armed opposition to the dictatorship, organized poetry readings throughout the United States in support of the Sandinista cause. Many celebrated poets, such as Lawrence Ferlinghetti and Allen Ginsberg, read at benefits for Nicaragua and later, after the Sandinista triumph in 1979, visited the homeland of Rubén Darío. Vargas is also the prime organizer of Ernesto Cardenal's historic first visit to the San Francisco Bay Area and the United States in 1976. It is during this visit to San Francisco that Ernesto Cardenal inaugurates the Mission Cultural Center with a campesino mass, followed by a mass baptism of some two hundred Mission District children, then a poetry reading of his own work.

During this period, Vargas's efforts are not just political, he also publishes in *Tin-Tan Magazine* his first work of fiction, "Sandino, 1925," his re-creation of the Nicaraguan hero's desire for a free homeland. At the height of the Sandinista insurrection, Vargas joins the Sandinista Front in Costa Rica and participates in the attack at Peñas Blancas in September 1978. After that he returns to San Francisco and rejoins the solidarity committee. Out of this experience comes—*Nicaragua, Yo Te Canto Besos Balas y Sueños de Libertad*.

The other important Nicaraguan poet of that decade is Pancho Aguila, who became a *cause célèbre* for many writers in the Bay Area. Pancho Aguila is the poet's *nom de guerre*, adopted when he was first jailed in the early 1970s. Pancho Aguila spent most of the decade of the '70s and part of the '80s incarcerated at Folsom Prison, where he was a key organizer of the Folsom Prison Writers' Workshop. In his life and his work, Aguila always considered himself a political prisoner, and the act for which he was jailed—bank robbery—a political crime. As could be expected, his work exhibits a strong political stance in favor of the oppressed and all political prisoners. The poems published by Second Coming Press in 1977 under the title *Dark Smoke* are typically angry, but within the anger, there are unmistakable gleams of hope and sincere humanity.

One other Nicaraguan poet published a book during this decade. Although Denis Corrales Martínez's book (a chapbook titled *Pinceladas Nicaragüenses*) did not have the impact or power of those of the two previously mentioned poets, it is important to note that his book was all in Spanish, whereas the other poets were writing in English. Corrales Martínez's work is characterized by the use of traditional verso of Hispanic literature, and also by his poetic concerns. Since he was a recent newcomer to San Francisco when he published this book (recent in comparison to Vargas and Aguila, who'd spent decades here), the poems are more traditionally Nicaraguan than Vargas's or Aguila's. The themes are the Nicaraguan workers, especially campesinos, and their oppression; the poems also emphasize the poet's concern for the environment and ecology.

Among other highlights of Central American writing in the Bay Area during this decade, I will cite two.

Born in Belize of Honduran parents and raised in Hollywood, California, Walter Alfredo Martínez's poetry and prose is written in classical formal English. His book, *Ascensions*, published in 1974 by Heirs Press in San Francisco, has the most surreal writing of this entire group of poets mentioned in this essay. The words skip and fly over the page, confronting the real world that the poet survives with ingenious imagination. The poet's concerns are the spirit and the soul—abstractions, to be sure, and yet the poems vibrate, tremble, dance, and engage the reader.

In 1975, Gilberto Osorio, a young Salvadorean artist-writer, publishes in *Tin-Tan Magazine* "Poesía in El Salvador," the first modern survey of Salvadoran poetry to appear in English. The essay, though written twenty-five years ago, is still a fine overview of Salvadoran writers from 1930 to 1974. Osorio is also instrumental in gathering the news of the death of Roque Dalton in 1975, which *Tin-Tan Magazine* publishes in issue number 2, October 1975. The magazine is the first to publish the news of the death of the Salvadorean poet in the United States.

HISTORICAL OVERVIEW OF THE 1980S

After 1979, the literary influence of Central Americans in San Francisco becomes predominantly Salvadoran, sparked in part by the political polarization of El Salvador, which causes large portions of the population to seek exile in the United States, and also in part by the Roque Dalton Cultural Brigade, a collective of writers, poets, and translators who take up the task of promoting Central American literature and poetry. Besides organizing poetry readings and cultural events that focus attention on El Salvador, the Roque Dalton Cultural Brigade also publishes three important books of Central American poetry in translation: *Volcán: Poems from Central America*; Otto René Castillo, *Tomorrow Triumphant*; and Roque Dalton, *Clandestine Poems*.

A few comments follow on these works. With *Volcán: Poems from Central America* (City Lights Books, 1983), for the first time in the United States, Central American poetry is released by an established publisher, which helps broaden the audience of this literature. But more important, the book introduces to United States readers the work of major poets such as Roque Dalton, Ernesto Cardenal, José Coronel Urtecho, Gioconda Belli, Claribel Alegría, Clementina Suárez, Claudia Lars, Roberto Paredes, Roberto Sosa, Daisy Zamora and many others.

The two other books translated by members of the Roque Dalton Cultural Brigade—*Tomorrow Triumphant* and *Clandestine Poems* reintroduce and enhance the reputation of Otto René Castillo and Roque Dalton within the United States.

By 1988, the Roque Dalton Cultural Brigade had ceased to exist, but several of its former members continue translating and contributing to the flowering of Central American writing during the 1990s.

It is not till 1989 that the first Salvadoran writers make their presence felt in the Bay Area. One is a novelist and the other the most prolific poet to emerge from the Central American diaspora in the Bay Area.

Jorge Argueta, besides being an active organizer of poetry and literary events during the late 1980s to the present, also publishes a body of work that is prolific, personal, and political.

Argueta publishes eighteen different collections of poetry between 1989 and the present, making him the most published of all the Central American writers in the Bay Area. The quality of the poetry is consistent and is characterized by its lyric quality, its brutal honesty, and its political perspective. The poetry is also often laced with humor and satire. The themes are abundant: traditional love between a man and a woman; untraditional love of prostitutes and street people; life in El Salvador; life in San Francisco; drug and alcohol binges; poems of desperation, anger, and hope; poems for children.

Argueta writes strictly in Spanish, but all his work is available in bilingual editions. Sometimes the poet translates his own work, such as in *Las Frutas del Centro*, and other times competent translators like Beatrice Hernandez and Barbara Jamison effectively bring the poet's voice across in English.

THE DECADE OF THE '90S

The decade of the 90s saw the first Central American woman writer achieve prominence in the Bay Area. A former school teacher, Martivón Galindo arrives in the Bay Area from her native land after being arrested and tortured by the security forces of El Salvador. She soon establishes herself as a writer and strong feminist voice. She goes on to graduate from the University of California at Berkeley. Her book *Retazos* combines prose vignettes and poems to recount her life as a child in El Salvador and her present condition as an exile in San Francisco. The writing is witty and engaging, and often presents the feminist side of love and politics.

In closing this section, I want to mention that translation of Central American authors also continued during the 1990s.

In particular, former members of the Roque Dalton Cultural Brigade published three volumes of translations—*Clamor of Innocence*, edited by Barbara Paschke and David Volpendesta, an anthology of short fiction from Central America; *Angel in the Deluge*, by Rosario Murillo, translated by the author; and *Riverbed of Memory*, by Daisy Zamora, translated by Barbara Paschke. All three volumes are published by City Lights Books in San Francisco.

The important publications of those decades, like *Tin-Tan Magazine*, *Gaceta Sandinista*, *El Pulgarcito*, and *El Tecolote*, a community newspaper that often publishes poetry, have added richly to the literary heritage of this city.

And even more recent in the flurry of poetry festivals launched in the Mission District, there was Flor y Canto en el Barrio 2008, sponsored by Friends of the San Francisco Public Library, a three-day festival of Latino poetry in the Mission District; and a few years later Flor y Canto en el Barrio, July 2011, a poetry festival on 24th Street. Both received wide support from the Mission District and from across the city.

In this brief catalogue of poets are the parallel literary histories of SF.

The truth is that we have never left San Francisco, we have just been left out. But now that we are on stage, now that our history is finally acknowledged, these currents and threads have come together—so that from now on, when we talk about the literary history of San Francisco, we can talk about the Beats, the non-Beats, the Mission poets, the Asian American poets, Afro-American poets, all of us singing the songs of our times and our place here in this beautiful city of poets. So after today we will no longer speak of parallel literary histories but of the literary history and heritage of San Francisco, punto final.

Nearly my entire literary life, except for my first published poem and my first public reading, has occurred in San Francisco or with San Francisco as my base. During this time I've had the privilege to publish other Latino poets such as the first books by José Montoya, Roberto Vargas, Nina Serrano, Elias Hruska-Cortes and raúlrsalinas; as editor of magazines such as *Tin-Tan Magazine*; as co-editor of anthologies such as *Time to Greez! Incantations from the Third World* (Glide Publications, 1974) and *Volcán: Poetry from Central America* (City Lights Books, 1984); and as a translator, including a book-length translation from the Spanish of Rosario Murillo's *Angel in the Deluge* (City Lights Books, 1993).

I have often been accused of being a poet and they're right, I am dangerous, I'm like a stepping razor, but the very first time I was accused it was, well, let me just read the poem—

The Poet Recalls His First Reading

Riding home from celebrating
my first book compadre riding shotgun
our lids heavy with poems and tequila
in beat-up sports car
crawling towards Bernal Heights
dawn a spider with a thousand legs of light

A black-and-white
flashing triple strobes
angry at Latinos
riding around this hour of morn
instead of heading to work
pulled us over

Compadre and I exchanged glances
as other encounters with billy clubs
handcuffs broken ribs surfaced from
our suddenly awake memories

Without license, nor any ID
I proved my name by reciting a poem
while badge 8601 dug my rhymes
and followed along in my proud book

Then 8601 returned to patrol car
while I winked at compadre thinking
we're cool with the heat so I never saw ol' 8601
slide up my window like a snake
put the 357 magnum to my temple
the barrel cold as a pinpoint of ice

The gun trembled in his hand
as his words pressed through lips tighter
than a chicken butt—You've a red warrant.
Move and I'll blow your damn head off.

I slanted my eyes at him and replied,
—Be cool. I'm not that bad a poet.

Now I hope that I haven't pissed off the American-Taliban-Industrial-Big-Pharma-Military Complex. But things being what they are—if one day I don't show up for my classes, you know where I'll be? I'm going to be in Cuba. Yes, that's right. A beautiful tropical island, with beautiful tropical people and beautiful tropical music everywhere you go. And that's going to be the good part. The bad part, of course, is that it is going to be in Guantánamo. So—if one day I don't show up, please contact your local representative.

Lorca's Dream

They tell me that your clavicle
is a star over Andalucía
that your melancholic metacarpals
still clutch a clod of earth in Sevilla
that your hips have not ceased dancing
in Havana like in Nueva York
that jasmines bloom in your eye sockets
and every petal a poem
that your jaw bone is the voice of all
the silenced ones, the undocumented ones
those insulted and executed
that the moon cradles your bones Federico
fragile as hummingbird wings

That's what I was told one silvery night
by the hip red ants
that sleep in your cranium

Now the nice thing about "Lorca's Dream" is that with
a few quick origami folds—and please don't try this at home
with your own poem—"Lorca's Dream" turns into a paper
airplane and then the dream itself flies off.

[The poet steps up to the edge of the stage and launches
the paper airplane poem into the audience.]

I don't know I just thought I'd try something different.

[Someone in the audience shouts for the poem to be
read in Spanish.]

Bueno, lo voy a leer in español porque el poema está
escrito así.

El sueño de Lorca

Me cuentan que tu clavícula
es una estrella sobre Andalucía
que tus melancólicos metacarpianos
aún aprietan un terrón de Sevilla
que tus caderas jamás
han cesado de gozar
así en La Habana como en New York
y que en las cuencas de tus ojos
han brotado jasmines
y cada pétalo un poema

que tu quijada es la voz de todos
los sospechosos, los indocumentados,
insultados y fusilados
que la luna arrulla tus hueso Federico
frágiles como alas de colibrí

Así me lo contaron una noche plateada
las hormiguitas rojas
que duermen en tu cráneo

I come to poetry out of necessity in a way, out of an urgent need to define who I am but also as a way to give voice to my community. To me poetry should be read out loud, and I encourage all of you to read to a poem to a friend and have a friend read one to you. To me poetry is how I stay alive, how I navigate the dark hours of the night.

My poetry is an impure poetry, a poetry that is accessible and that you don't need a professor of literary theory to deconstruct for you. In fact, I think my poetry resists deconstruction, because it is not goofing around, or playing games with language but rather, like my friend said the other day "There's not one extra word in it."

Because poetry, after all, as the poet once said, is the best word in the best place.

My work is at times bilingual or multilingual, and sometimes doesn't give a lingual or lengua how it expresses itself as long as it remains true to the word as Eduardo Galeano says. And to paraphrase one of the great writers of our times, to think that poetry can change the world is absurd, but to think that the world can be changed without poetry is equally absurd.

For me—poetry is also prophecy, language fused to prophecy, that's poetry. So let's take the language about a particular debate going on about immigration reform: Folks, 12 million Latinos in the United States are not illegal, nor undocumented—but rather refugees.

Without having to retell the litany of woes that is the history of U.S.-Latin American relations, a current example will do. Two years ago the Obama administration through Secretary of State Hillary Clinton basically launched another coup d'état, this time in Honduras. What this golpe de estado did was to support the corrupt, decrepit oligarchy that has decimated the country for the past two hundred years. And now we can see the benefits of that coup—Honduras has now become the most violent country on earth. More homicides and violent deaths per thousand than Iraq, Afghanistan, West Oakland or La Misión. So what our government has done is burn down the house of Honduras. How many thousands and thousands of refugees did this violence create? Refugees that fled that fire and are now here in this country.

So here's my prophecy—let's call it the Poet Laureate Prophecy. It doesn't matter how high, how wide or how long you make that border fence—as long you keep burning down the houses of Latin America, refugees will keep coming.

Now that I've gotten that off my chest I guess it is time for a love poem.

Aquí con tu memoria

Hoy me senté pensativo
mirando al mar
atado como prisionero
a otro día
enroscado
hecho caracol
por todo lo fecundo que eres
en esta tierra y este mar
el chillido de las gaviotas
las nubes como reflexión del agua
el cielo como tu caricia ese día de junio
del cual ha quedado
sólo este momento—
estos segundos donde surges otra vez del mar
tu traje de baño silueta de pura espuma
espléndida, joven, sirena de brazos bronceados
pelo color de arena quemada
mujer hecha de embrujos, de flores acuáticas
de tierra, montaña, yerbas
que ahora son poema
porque estuvimos juntos esa tarde
y los dos fuimos hechos calendarios
donde se retornan siempre los días
con sus mismos destinos
los mismos amores y enemigos de siempre
solo tú y yo quedamos
porque fuimos

chorro de agua, música,
el rubí de un beso
cayendo hacia el fondo de un pozo
donde a través de los años
nos miramos como éramos aquel día
pobres y enamorados del mundo entero

I want to dedicate this next poem to my longtime col-
leagues and big supporters of my work, Jack Hirschman and
Agneta Falk, and in memory of Roque Dalton.

A Poem for my Hat

> For Jack Hirschman and Agneta Falk
> In memory of Roque Dalton

Today I'm going to wear a hat
step out on my porch
in a friendly floppy one
and wave hello to the world
Or maybe a mysterious fedora, brim down low
Investigate the missing Brown Buffalo
Perhaps a Greek fisherman's hat—a song to the briny
    deep—
the sirens and mermaids at my shoulder rocking me
Oh—a big old Mexican sombrero would do
with silver thread along the edge
that will hurt because of you
A tropical white Panama, woven by hundred-year-old hands

with a parrot feather on the band
and I'll dance some slick mambos
I could sport a krazy kat hat with balloons and milagritos
on the crown and stroll down Mission Street
leading a lobster on a leash
I could style a brown beret—cocked over angry eyebrow
and shout Power to the People and other slogans I forget

Maybe I'll try a cloud with a blue ribbon
tied around it like a song
Or none of that—
Today I'm going to wear the sky as my hat
and then I'll pass it on to you
so you can wear it too

Because the poet laureateship belongs to all of us—it is
my intention to make this city the poetic center of the Amer-
icas, a city where poetry, poetry readings, poetry workshops
and poetry festivals blossom everywhere people work and
gather, in schools and libraries, in detention centers, so that
hope might spring from poetry, in government offices, the
Board of Supervisors, even the Mayor's office, because poetry
demands an honest voice, expressed in clear language that is
true to the word—who better to have a poetry workshop
than the Board of Supervisors. I would be thrilled for poetry
to have such an impact that the political leaders of the future
would also be judged by the condensed thought of their hai-
kus, the wit of their epigrams, and the truth of their words.
Let all politicians and citizens of San Francisco from now on

be measured by their knowledge of poetry, the uniqueness of their poetic vision.

Here are some of the projects I would like to achieve during my tenure. But also keep in mind I have been approached by others—but they have to take it upon themselves also. A Flor y Canto Youth Festival, which we will roll out in the coming weeks. Poetry in public spaces like bus stops, Muni shelters, inside buses, outside buses, poetry on murals all over the city. If we are lucky we will follow up on the fine work of [former] Poet Laureate Jack Hirschman to continue the International Poetry Festival, and maybe expand it by becoming a sister city with Barcelona. And lastly I would like to launch a project where important literary sites in the Mission and throughout the city are identified with bronze plaques commemorating the poet or their work.

I don't know if anyone saw this big huge cannonball of a man hanging out in the lobby before the event. But that was the Brown Buffalo—I had a chance to say hello but he didn't want to stay, cause he's been on his own Brown Buffalo run for many years. But the Brown Buffalo wrote one of the great novels of United States literature, *The Revolt of the Cockroach People*—and he wrote it in the Royan Hotel, "the Mission's finest."

The first site I am going to request a plaque for is outside the Royan Hotel commemorating Oscar Zeta Acosta's history.

This poem is about my neighborhood and starts by mentioning three important poets—if you don't know their work, check it out.

16th & Valencia

I saw Jack Micheline reciting Skinny Dynamite
on the corner of 16th & Valencia
and he was angry
and the next day he was dead
on the last BART train to Concord
and maybe that's why he was angry
I met Harold Norse shuffling around in a beaten world
his pockets stuffed with poems only hipsters read
It's a cesspool out here he sighed
before retreating to his room in the Albion Hotel
where angels honeycomb the walls with dreams
and the rent is paid with angry poems
I heard Oscar Zeta Acosta's brown buffalo footsteps
pounding the Valencia Corridor
and he was shouting poetry at the sick junkies
nodding with their wasted whores
in the lobby of the Hotel Royan "The Mission's finest"
and even the furniture was angry
I joined the waiters at the bus stop
the waitresses the norteño trios the flower sellers
the blind guitarist wailing boleros at a purple sky
the shirtless vagrant vagabond ranting at a parking meter
the spray-paint visionary setting fire to the word
and I knew this was the last call
We were tired of living from the scraps of others
We were tired of dying for our own chunk of nothing
And I saw this barrio as a freight train

a crazy Mexican bus careening out of control
a mutiny aboard a battleship
and every porthole filled with anger
And we were going to stay angry
And we were not leaving
Not ever leaving
El corazón del corazón de La Misión
El Camino Real ends here!

My literary history is not just the Mission and the Latino community but I embrace the entire city. The Mission, the Outer Mission, Bernal Heights, Potrero Hill, the Bayview, even Pacific Heights, and, of course, North Beach, the first Latino barrio of the city. I'm also a big supporter of the Revolutionary Poets Brigade, which is the most important group right now, a group that has taken poetry from being a passive art to an active art. And even now, in the twenty-first century, I think the echo is there of the Roque Dalton Cultural Brigade.

The Eyes of the Poet
For Bob Kaufman

Corrugated iron panels
stamped on your forehead
your eyes two pennies rattling
in a blind man's cup/ yet once
the sharpest Beat on the scene

of New York tenement parties/ later
tales of Tangiers/ white slavery
amphetamine dreams/ snow in August/ jazz
jazz on your breakfast plate/ and jailhouse riffs
etched with a silver razor/ somehow a busted nose
then named Prince of Poetry/ a black Rimbaud
sailing bamboo raft into exile and silence
a baby buddha perched on your shoulder
blowing a saxophone dirge
    down
    your river Nile

To follow in the footsteps of Lawrence Ferlinghetti, the grandfather of all of us, Janice Mirikitani, the great Asian-American poet; of devorah major, the voice of the Afro-American community; Jack Hirschman, with *The Arcanes*; and Diane di Prima, with *Revolutionary Letters*, is a heavy act to follow, and I am humbled, honored and proud to serve you as your next poet laureate.

And as the beating heart of American poetry, in the continental sense dreamed of by José Martí, I would propose that we adopt as the most honorable address to a fellow citizen of San Francisco, the City of Poets of the Americas—not doctor, or esquire, not even mayor, or supervisor—but the most honorific and respectful way to address a fellow human being—Poeta!

Before I go I would like to thank Lawrence Ferlinghetti, Jack Hirschman, Agneta Falk, Nancy Peters at City Lights, Elaine Katzenberger, Peter, Stacey, Paul, everyone at City Lights for their support, José B. Cuellar and Jorge Molina, the Peña-Govea family, my friend the Honduran poet Walter Martinez, who first turned me on to Lorca and César Vallejo, Dona Baro, Daniel del Solar from *Tin-Tan Magazine*, raúlrsalinas, Jorge Argueta and Luna's Press, Randy Fingland and CC. Marimbo Press, Meredith May, Byron Spooner and the Friends of the Library, Joan Jasper and Michelle Jeffers, City Librarian Luis Herrera, the Nomination Committee and Mayor Ed Lee, for taking the risk in the Year of the Dragon. My sister Livier and brother-in-law Tom, my compadre Roberto Vargas, my late brother Raymond who first turned me on to banned books, and of course, again, Magaly y Marisol, all my relations and all of you for supporting poetry, literature and literacy.

Before I close with a final poem—I'll leave you with these last thoughts: Never forget that San Francisco is the city of poets—therefore, each and every one of you is a poet until proven otherwise.

There's No Santos on My Altar

Sometimes I wonder Ché
If you ever grew tired of being up on the altar
If you ever got weary of being the pure one el hombre nuevo

I wonder if you ever thought of just being Ché again
The one with a girlfriend who abandoned you
When you rode the Norton 500 across the Andes like a crazy
    beat

Whatever happened to that frustrated poet who
Instead became a revolutionary who'd wished he'd been a
poet
And at the risk of sounding ridiculous was a poet

Didn't you ever miss a tango by Piazzola
In that faded blue light of Buenos Aires at five p.m.
When drunken love songs fill the porteño barrios

Or was it all strategy, tactics, central committees
The politics of rhetoric
A mouthful even for a poet

Your diary in Bolivia is stained with mud and shit
But it is also stained with hope

You made your share of mistakes
You forgot god damn it the necessity to tango
You failed to read The Garden of Forking Paths

You were right about love and revolution and wrong
About most everything else—in other words you were human

So tonight another anniversary of your death
I'm sure somewhere someplace in Cuba the Congo Vietnam
Chiapas
A hungry bastard with nothing but hope in his gut

Will light a candle at your portrait
Surely it will be the one with a red star on your beret—
Your eyes staring with nostalgia at the future

But Ché I have no santos on my altar
No idols no gods no goddesses
Only flower petals and hummingbird feathers

So instead of a candle I'll play you a tango
One that starts with a ráfaga of bandoneón
Like the roar from a motorcycle and with my canteen

That survived the Southern Front in Nicaragua back in 1979
I'll tip you a toast hombre a hombre—Amor vino y revolución
Ché comandante presente!

Yo soy Alejandro Murguía—y no me parezco a nadie.

STRAY
POEMS

Ahora Fuego

Ha llegado la rebelión de colores
insurreción de palabras
Es la hora carnal
así dice el tic-toc del tiempo

Es la temporada de ayunas
el mes de los mendigos
la zafra de lágrimas
tiene sabor a coraje
a sal, a miel de alacrán

Es el año del viento
un siglo de sangre que se forma
un huracán de gente
avanzando por los callejones
y arrabales
hacia el centro
comandando la ópera del capitalismo
la farsa del imperialismo
—dando fin al cinismo y mentiras

Es el minuto donde se hunden
los buques de guerra
el segundo donde se ahoga
la injusticia, la deuda, la renta, la tiranía—

Fire Now

It's the rebellion of the colors
the insurrection of the words
It's time carnal
that's what the tic-toc of the clock says

It's the season of fasting
the orchard of the wretched
the harvest of tears
has a taste of anger
salt, scorpion honey

It's the century of wind
a year of blood
a hurricane of people
storming from the alleys
and slums
towards the center
knocking over the soap opera of capitalism
the farce of imperialism
putting an end to cynicism and lies

It is the minute
when battleships sink
the second when
injustice, debt, rent, tyranny, dictatorships drown

Es la hora hermana de los fósforos
de las llamaradas y el fuego

Llegó el tiempo
De la Hora Cero

It's the month for the matches my sister
of the flames and the fire

It is time
Zero Hour has come

Cuatro Copas

Cuatro copas en la barra
se preguntan una a una
si la luna es nuestra o es ajena.
Cuatro copas menos una
y cada una que queda
dice como broma
Lunar, luna, una
sobre el mar tranquilo
donde el faro alumbra la playa
Y ahora quedan dos copas y faltan dos
y las dos que quedan
se olvidan que fueron cuatro
Y los amigos lejanos
como los barcos cruzando el mar
bajo la luna—
Luna que mira por las rejas
de la barra
la última copa que queda
Y la copa se pregunta
¿Y los amores y los amigos?
esta noche tan noche
se han olvidado de mí
como se olvidan los ricos de los pobres.
Y sólo queda esta sola copa
el recuerdo y el olvido
de lo que fui y lo que he vivido
Cuatro copas en la barra

Four Cups

Four cups on the bar
ask each other
if the moon is ours or belongs to others.
Four cups minus one
and every one of them
says jokingly
one mole moon
over the calm sea
where a lighthouse lights the beach
And now there's two cups left
and two cups missing
and the two remaining forget
they were once four
And distant friends
like ships crossing the sea beneath the moon
moon that peeks through
the rails of the bar
at the last cup left
And this cup asks itself
and my loves and my friends
this night so night
have forgotten me
like the rich forget the poor.
And there's only this last lonely cup—
memory and longing
of what I've been and what I've lived
Four cups on the bar

los últimos amigos
de un bohemio en una noche
en una ciudad sin nombre
far, far away
tan lejos, lejos
como la luna

   —San Cristóbal de las Casas, 8 de Agosto, 2008

the last friends of this bohemian
tonight, in a nameless city
lejos, muy lejos
as far, far away
as the moon

        —San Cristóbal de las Casas, August 8, 2008

Tango Roto

A slice of moonlight, a pool of blood, an exiled tango. The click-click of high heels along a tree-lined avenue, traces of lipstick on a half-smoked cigarette, the mournful sigh of a moody bandoneón escaping from an opened window, ice melting in a champagne bucket, her purple beret, the fragrance of crushed gardenias lingering between white bed sheets, an aged bohemian in an empty café calling for his cognac, a sullen foghorn in the mist-draped harbor, an aimless cab ride through barrio streets, the corner where two men once knifed each other over a vulgar phrase said in lunfardo and a scratchy record of Carlos Gardel singing "Volver." The last train from Buenos Aires, the trampling of hobnailed boots in La Plaza de Mayo, a blood-soaked shirt left at an army barracks, icicles hanging on barbed wire like bayonets, a canceled passport, the memory of wine on her mouth—midnight—an eerie siren, an unanswered phone in a dimly lit police station ringing and ringing, steel-gray clouds floating across an endless sky, a creased black and white photograph hidden between the pages of a book.

You never know who will appear with your abandoned
    baggage.

Adiós muchachos.

Havana by Night

Like tropical flowers washed ashore by a hurricane
Jineteras are lush tonight on the teeming streets of Havana
High-waisted girls poured into tightly cropped shorts
They spill out of taxis hotels bars or the malecón
Their red glossy lips a calling card imported from 1958
They curse fluently in three languages
Even as they draw the foreign tricks
"Quieres una mujer?" "Voulez vous coucher avec moi?"
    "You want a date?"
She'll do anything for a pair of jeans or a five-dollar bill
Her profile tight as a sail her voice like a schoolgirl's
"Fuck me any way you want come in my ass even my face."
(By day she nurses a clinic where they're so strapped for
    medicine
You'd think there was a goddamn blockade going on)
Her shoulders soft as coconut cream, she whispers as you
    touch her
"I've had nothing to eat all day."
In the Hotel Nacional the conga band is pounding
With such fury as if to sink Miami into the sea
And the hungry *jinetera* rolls her hips hallucinating
A full-serve cafeteria across the street from where she lives

Report from Hell's Living Room

Don't enter—I should tell you
I am not responsible, I'm not
I'm only the reporter
you can see for yourself
what I have found
in the last room
at the end of the hall

You must leave the ivy-covered walls
step outside the deceptive houses
you cannot believe if you stay behind those windows
you cannot see unless you stare at the shadows
catch the light from the street
the barely seen silhouettes
of human forms

The scene is gruesome, so you've been warned
bodies everywhere—stabbed, shotgunned, knifed, strangled
slashed in the throat, bashed in the head
a skull split in half down to the nose
death without dignity
legs apart, dresses up their crotch
or pants dropped to the ankle
but sometimes with style—the suicide noose
knotted clean as a tie
and here too someone writes the common letters
that record their foreign-sounding Latino names

the awkward words
that tell us their race, their origin

They were women, men
everyday people whose lives mock us
you can tell by the details
the shoes they wear
the clothes
the claustrophobic rooms
places you would commit murder
just to move out

It came sudden, it came violent
sometimes carefully planned
one thing you can say is that words cut
precise as razors
and later you must remember
parts of the body
not meant to be seen
bone, heart, gut
and keep these words close
because they are honest as life or death

You don't want to lie about this
you can't cheat
dishonest words are shit

Let me be clear as aguardiente
the struggle was fierce

blood all over the room is proof
we all look the same when dead
that same funny mummy smile
or our eyes half-closed
not wanting the last instant to end

I didn't see them do it
I came later but count the wounds
the stink was fresh / the same
with dead words and mutilated bodies
books without pages

I'm only reporting from the scene
standing in the death room
a towel on my face
noting every word that is alive

Resurrection Easter 1999

Incense candles *llantos* midnight mass
Orthodox Church of the Ascension 14th & Valencia
worshippers celebrate the rebirth of man
the rebirth of spirit the rebirth—KRISTOS ENESTIS—
bearded orthodox priest raises chalice to man
crucified "This is my body, this is my blood"
while outside heroin refugees shoot up
a blessed fix—ashes to ashes dust to dust
Easter 1999 weary masses of Kosovo trek
through mountain paths cutting new Trail of Tears
(old ones not yet dried Wounded Knee 1896
massacre of Sioux families by US Cavalry) refugees
in the footsteps of other refugees (Hellenes 1456)
the trail winds till the last refugee finds their way home
Armenia 1911 how many millions massacred?
The Treaty of Lausanne 1922 three million displaced
        overnight
Refugees never forget—The holy wine and loaves offered
I drink from this cup
I eat of this fleshy bread
xopilotes whirling over the sacrifice
a phone call brings the feared news—
Your uncle's dead your cousin's killed your sister's raped
Your mother your father your grandparents your house
        burned
even the cow is dead there's nothing left of your village

but ashes ashes dust dust blowing through satellites in outer
    space
(This Easter in Califas three tourists killed in Yosemite
and in Wyoming a gay man crucified on a lonely road)
We have lost our collective minds/ We have forgotten
when we kill another we kill ourselves bit by bit
Klinton bombs Kosovo Easter 1999 Hitler bombed Belgrade
Easter 1941 the Brits massacred the Irish Easter 1916
Cortez lands in Vera Cruz Easter 1519 and burns
    Tenochtitlán/
Refugees never forget
Birth death resurrection/ mother offers her newborn on the
    altar
the sacrificial lamb desired by the mad gods of war
and in somber Easter night of 1999 Kosovo burns
Belgrade burns/ a thousand villages burn in the mountains
of our century/ we are death, the destroyers—give us our
    daily bombs
our guided missiles our long distance destruction brought
    to us
by the miracle of brain dead talking heads by the
    ambassadors
of Pepsi and Big Macs the new centurions the new legions
invading the world/ million dollar missiles prop the
    ekonomy
reports wall street journal unemployment is down
the dow-jones is up to 10000 points the week Belgrade
is bombed/ business is booming and what's good for
    business

is good for who started the war in Kosovo/ follow the trail
of oil and you will reach the castle of war/ name who
covets uranium and you will name the generals of genocide
(Monika where have you gone now that we need you
to blow peace into the president?) Refugees never forget
Addis Abba 1936 Madrid 1938 Shanghai 1940
the Crying Songs were brought to Greece in the exodus of
    1922
the Emperor Justinian destroyed the Greek temples 600 AD
the Persians still curse Alexander for burning Persopolis
    300 BC
the memory of refugees is longer than the road they travel
across centuries and millennia now new
refugees are cowering under the missiles of Adolf Klinton
and on Easter Sunday morning B-1 bombers
rain grief and chaos on a city with a history longer
than the United States/ Death rebirth resurrection/
from Afghanistan to El Salvador
ashes you shall rise/ burned villages you shall rise/ grain
you shall rise/ corn of Chiapas/ scorched fields of Kosovo
burned apartments of Belgrade you shall rise and be
    reborn—
let the dead bury their dead and let the living get on with it
The priest chants and the people chant in the smoky
    cathedral
while the dawn of the Resurrection is shattered by the roar
of F-15 fighters/ Christ rising through Kosovo morning
is brought down by missile barrage (like video game)
just another heart on the altar/ Our own house is on fire

and we are watching it burn to the ground/ father kisses
      daughter on forehead
Will they know peace in their lifetimes?
In the Cathedral of the Ascension the prayers go on
the bombing goes on through the long night of missiles
refugees from all over the world are pounding on our doors
and we must let them eat from the bread of life
Refugees never forget ANASTASIS ANASTASIS

Not Flag Nor Country

Not flag nor country
can cover the dead boy in the rubble
the woman maimed at the check point
the village bombed—life deformed.
For a flag and country without god
because god does not take sides
nor parcel out land or oil
because god is not a century 21 real estate agent
because god has no flag or country
For flag and country and united fruit company
and chevron-texaco and enron and on and on
and millions in profits for wall street and for
        flag&country.com
For flag and country and racial purity
Sand Creek, Wounded Knee, Treblinka, Manzanar, Sabra &
        Shatila
For flag and country and abstract shit
—like flag and country
Better a country of oceans, mountains,
rivers and ravines, indescribable clouds,
hummingbirds and a chorus of flowers
Better a rock than a flag
Better a palm's breadth of nothing
than go armed for country
Better a country where prisons are outlawed
where schools are free *and* exciting
And poetry MAN-DA-TO-RY

—For police and politicians
Better a country for all—for you & we & us
with a flag made of words that are true
and said with corazón
A flag for all humanity
all of us under it
living and working and making love
or just to see old age respected
and to die with dignity
Rather this—or no flag, no country
neither flag nor country
THE DEAD ARE NOT IN MY NAME
That's not my god-damn-fucking flag
That's not my mother-fucking-country country

Big Girls Don't Cry

I warned you it'd be tough
Loving a man like me
Someone dangerous, with rough hands
That want to squeeze your tender waist
A man who absent five months
Shows up without calling, just appears
On your porch, ringing your doorbell
And wants all of you—
Now, this instant,
As if he owned you
On the hallway carpet
Or the kitchen table, who smokes
Cohibas when he's talking
And spits them out when he's done
A man who doesn't know how to lose
Won't take no and yes is calamitous
A rogue, an outlaw, a pirate
Who still sleeps with his ex-wife
But calls you his buti babe muñeca
Then leaves at dawn a fugitive
Without a word goodbye because
You said you were a big girl
Knew what you were getting into
I told you it'd be hard
Now come here and kiss me

Hombre Mucho Malo

I have gone out in high noon sun
faced off John Wayne cowboys
never backed up from a good fight
now alone I ride into smoggy sunset
dogs bark at me they know I'm bad
goody two-shoes throw rocks and palos
call me hombre mucho malo

I was an enemy of the secret police
The fbi, cia, cointelpro
ripped off banks and rich boys' toys
the only black hat in a sea of white
you see me coming so get set
moms are worried but virgins are hmm . . .
Godzilla wants me mano a mano
hombre mucho malo

Soy el chin en chingón
hago lo que me da la pinchi gana
hombre-mucho-fucking-malo
es que no me parezco a nada

I slung caló, slang, cussed, even punned
pissed on the president and all his boys
with no apologies and no regrets
there is no flowers for the bad

no rest in peace no sweet good–byes
hermano I lived the only life I had
hombre mucho malo

Mission Vision

I'm from the Mission
And I'm on a mission
like you're on a mission
and we are on a mission
and the mission is
to be in the Mission
Me entiendez, Mendez?

La Misión, La Mission, The Mission
wherever I stand
here, there, everywhere
I'm in the Mission
and the Mission is in me
like the Mission is in you
because the mission is to be in the Mission

Spectators, operators, speculators
all roaming the Mission
but there's some people missing from La Misión, qué no?

Watch your watch when you're in the Mission
Check the descarga beat on Mission Street
because the heat is on the Mission
so the mission now has to be
to free the Mission
Yes, hear me straight everyone

that's the vision
and what a vision

Free the Mission
That's the mission
Free the Mission
Ho!

Aquí con tu memoria

Hoy me senté pensativo
mirando al mar
atado como prisionero
a otro día
enroscado
hecho caracol
por todo lo fecundo que eres
en esta tierra y este mar
el chillido de las gaviotas
las nubes como reflexión del agua
el cielo como tu caricia ese día de junio
del cual ha quedado
sólo este momento—
estos segundos donde surges otra vez del mar
tu traje de baño silueta de pura espuma
espléndida, joven, sirena de brazos bronceados
pelo color de arena quemada
mujer hecha de embrujos, de flores acuáticas
de tierra, montaña, yerbas
que ahora son poema
porque estuvimos juntos esa tarde
y los dos fuimos hechos calendarios
donde se retornan siempre los días
con sus mismos destinos
los mismos amores y enemigos de siempre
solo tú y yo quedamos
porque fuimos

Here with Your Memory

Today I sat down pensive
staring at the sea
pinned like a prisoner
to another day
curled up
made a conch
by all fecund things you are
on this earth and in this sea
the cry of seagulls
the clouds like a reflection of the water
the sky like your caress that June day
of which the only thing left is this moment
these seconds when you surge again
out of the sea
your bathing suit pure foam
splendid, young mermaid
with bronzed arms
hair the color of burnt sand
woman made of spells, aquatic flowers
of earth, mountains, herbs
made into poems
because we were together that afternoon
and were transformed into calendars
where the days always return
with their same destinies
the same lovers and enemies as always
only you and I

chorro de agua, música,
el rubí de un beso
cayendo hacia el fondo de un pozo
donde a través de los años
nos miramos como éramos aquel día
pobres y enamorados del mundo entero

because we were
a gush of water, music,
the ruby of a kiss
falling into the depths
where across all the years
we see each other
as we were that day
poor and in love with the whole world.

El Arete

During our last fight
I threw one of your
Mexican silver earrings
Out the window
Where the street swallowed it
Breaking forever the pair
You loved so much
And I did it
So you'd never wear them
For another man

Detalles

What matters is the particulars
the precise meaning in your words:
—I love the specificity of detail

January drenched
with lemon blossoms
your hip pressing mine
your smile predicting rain
the sassy diction of your walk
in black leather jacket
supple and sexy as your hair
but I didn't surrender
till you snapped open red umbrella
and my heart flew out like a butterfly

our hotel window looked out to the bay
bridge lights were prismed in your eyes
how your black seamed stockings
flowed like crazy punctuation
to my hand prints on your ass
the profane unction of our act
holy when performed by lovers
your happy cry and my sad laughter
twined in a wax calendar
your whispered vow before an altar
of hummingbirds and paper corazones
—I will never leave you.

Never.

Minor details of our bruised affair.
The anklet with my name
in what drawer do you keep it?

Warning at Noon

The air raid siren
bursts upon the day
heralding nuclear destruction
and the end of entertainment
          as we know it

What is the use of this world—
as I come upon your
note, your handwriting
still legible though a bit
faded and erased
by the tyranny of your absence

What good is it
to remember you
when the backwards
race of humanity
has sprung Armageddon
this afternoon
          this Tuesday

so I tear up your note
and continue emptying
          my desk drawers

Persuasion (All the Reasons Why)

Because it had to be you/ it could only be me

because it's one of those crazy things

porque eres mi sagrada tentación/ porque en mis noches te
    sueño

because you ask the right question/ because you're pyramid and
    ziggurat

porque amor indio chula/ porque sos cihuatl-xochitl

because your splendid legs/ porque te pones como gata

because your sheer black stockings/ because I dress you and
    undress you

porque te apodo La Consentida/ porque eres ingrata y
    traicionera—

pues que wacha ruka Chicano style/ porque soy del barrio
    ésa

porque seras mi huisa/ porque te dicen La Más Chingona

porque llevo tatuado tu nombre en mis brazos

porque eres mi historia y mi destino/

porque sos mi frente de guerra/ porque serás mi Celaya

porque me duele saber que fuiste ajena/ porque siempre
    seras mía

because to love this way is dangerous & could make any
    man bitter

porque soy tu amargura/ porque eres Doña Dulzura

because you have the sassiest walk I've ever seen

because your red stiletto heels/ because your corset and eyes

because I possess you front and back/ because at three or
    four a.m.

the rough play the leather and the latex

because you whisper my name/ because I'm an orchid in
your mouth

porque sabes a agua de coco/ because you're my tropic of
desire

because you're a Coptic manuscript I must decipher

because I decipher you/ porque eres clásica y sensual

because my hat hurts when I think of you/ porque te quiero
verde

because your words are like stones/ because you slash the
accent of my name

because you don't give a tit/ because you're midnight sun

and August snow roses in December

because in spite of everything you read my steamy letters

because you'd do anything for me A-NY-THING even
Murder you say

because you make me laugh/ because you're the nails in a
Frida painting

porque eres el último bolero de mi última parranda

porque así lo quiero así me gusta/ porque me da la chingada
gana

porque no me parezco a nadie/ porque te adoro como una
santa

porque eres mi virgen y mi puta/ porque eres la mera mera
la pura neta

because you're mine and I know it/ porque eres película
Mexicana

porque soy tan melodramático

because you put up with me/ porque—yo no sé por qué?

Porque a pesar de todo me perdonas mis pecados me
    perdonas
todos mis pecados/ because you step inside the square ring
    with me
because you fight me with Marx and lingerie/ because I
    don't know
who'll win/ because you're ritual and magic/ luz y sombra/
    sol y luna
because I understand you/ because you're a mystery I can't
    solve
because our contradictions unite us
because nuestra cosa es más que locura
because you are the last woman for me in this life
because I want it this way/ because I don't give a damn
because nothing can separate us/ because we'll always be
    apart
because I could never describe it to you/ because
you're everything I want/ because
I'll never have you/ because such is life así es la vida
that's just how it is—porque el destino lo quiso así
porque piensa en mí mami/ porque pienso en ti
porque hoy y mañana ayer y siempre/ because the future is
    almost gone
because our time is so brief and absence is so so long
because it's now or never without regrets always and forever
                                        Pues baby así es

Three Seeds for Your Birthday

For sure you can track me down not that I've been hiding
Find the place I sleep and wedge into my dreams
Your owl wings flapping on my chest
The scent of clay and dust on your feathers
Your candy kiss no different than La Pelona's
Since you both wish me cempazúchitls on my headboard
And in your kinder moods a whirlwind of destruction

Yes you can place your hands upon my eyes
Blind me like Delilah does order exile to the salt mines
Give me sand to drink on the reservation
Pray that quicksand will swallow me
Or the FBI clamp me in chains
But what's the point since you get no pleasure from it

I can do the same—make this poem a jungle
A guerrilla column sent to rescue me
A parrot on my wrist or a monkey on your shoulder
Confuse you with backward footprints
Crumb trails that spin in circles
Hocus pocus
Unlisted phone number phony email address
Fake Facebook page
Only I don't want to waste my time

Watch out what you wish for doesn't bite you
You'll have clouds in your coffee and a life of sorrow

I'll take your bitterness and turn it into kindness
Send you this poem and kisses on your birthday
A silver cross from Chalma with opals from the desert
Plus these seeds—calabaza tomate chile
And rain to make them grow

María Ophelia

María Ophelia moves through shadows
In Echo Lake Park—her children
Close beside her she leads them
With pencils in their hands
To the water where jade fish swim
And her worker lover has not returned tonight

An ancient holy man once crossed a desert
And learned there are no borders
Just the empty hearts of men
And he said that everyone is alone—
But none more alone than the refugee
In the dismal factories of LA

María Ophelia looks into the lake
Where her children sleep like tadpoles dreaming
The rock garden is painted malachite
The green moonlight pulls trolleys up Angel's Flight
Serpentine roses whisper her name
To the frozen wind
And María Ophelia sleeping in the gloomy waters
Of Echo Lake Park paper straws in her hair
Pop-top lids on her eyes
—No llores María Ophelia
Your daughters can learn at school today
The teacher won't turn them in to La Migra
María Ophelia the hospital is safe and open

You can walk the streets in daylight
You can step out of the shadows
No llores María Ophelia no llores—
No llores más María Ophelia
No llores más.

The Cigarettes, the Beers, the Trash

Everything is good for something
Even the trash, the ugly and the dirty,
What we throw away we can put in a poem,
Make art of our rejections, our defeats
All of it just grist for the mill of our songs.

It's too bad that sometimes we want only the pretty,
That which makes us believe we're saints, or holy,
Or some kind of artiste, for hell's sake.

Send me storms when I'm walking home
Locusts in the harvest season
I'd rather go hungry than
Stuff my gills at some catered banquet
Where everyone is neutered by Martha Stewart.

Look outside your frigging window,
What you see is what it is—that's all there is.
I see abandoned cars, newspapers, a beer bottle
Propped up against a half-dead tree
And I'm going to put them in this poem
Because that's all I've got tonight.

Then I'll smoke a cigarette, stare at the night clouds,
Let the wind whip my face
    And that's it, at least I'll know I didn't cheat,
                        Didn't fake what's in my life.

Tequila Song

If you drink enough tequila
you will become an honorary Mexican
and may be stopped for identification

If I Go Down

This one is for every motherfucker that tried to fuck me
For every fat banker's ass that tried to ride me
For every hobnail-booted nazi that tried to crush me
This one is for you and it ain't no dud, dude

This goes out to the politico hypocrite hemorrhoid of
    society
For the righteous child-rapist in the pulpit
For the bloodsucking multinational digging their fangs into
    my groin
For the dealer-doper-rip-off artist injecting poisonous
    mercury into
my neighborhood
This one is for you
And I'm writing it with care

For the skull-eyed goon of every hamlet
and backwater outpost on this planet
For the helmeted viper with bayonet to a woman's throat
For the ball-less cabrón who set fire to my house with
    napalm
For every fascist racist punk who ever hurled a rock through
    a window
For the wall street speculator who put a price on dreams
Yes, you know who you are—this proem fits you like a
    leather collar

For every hijo de la gran puta who ever asked for my green
        card, my ID card, my passport, my registration, my
        driver's license, my insurance, my fees
For every suit and tie bastard who's after me to pay up
For the tax collector, bill collector, overdue bill collector
For the courts in all their vicious mayhem
For the sheriffs, the judges and the juries
Who sentence me without possibility of life
To all of them and at the same time
It's a quarter past three in the morning
The wind is howling up a storm
It's bitter out here in the streets
And no chump mayor is going to tell me
it ain't so
But I'll survive this night I swear
As for those pig-fuckers
grinning up in their privileged lofts
along with all the rest
who would like to see me eat shit
let me tell you this—if I go down
even on my knees I'll ram my fist
two feet up your arse

occupy this

occupy means
a space
that is yours
like this poem is yours
so light it on fire—
hurl it drenched
in caustic wit
at the corrupt mummies
that suffocate words
in the language of profits
stock averages indexes
hedge funds

ram this poem like a spear
in the cycloptic eye of greed
crunch it up and sling it
to break down wall street
spread it out for shelter when the rains come
sail it as a raft to save your sweetie
from the storm
read it at a park in a voice
999,000 strong

this poem is pregnant
it can be anything

even a paper plane
to fly you into exile

so go ahead—just do it
occupy this poem

The Dark Side of the Light
For Lenny Bruce

You know this guy
Standing outside the norm
Hip before hip was born
Solid to his fingertips
His voice like a razor
Sharp and deadly
And eyes, eyes like butterflies
And words cyanide on the tongue

You know this guy
Dressed in black
A monkey on his back
And 14 gashes on his arm
A cross dangling from his chest
And Moses on his lips
That's how it goes when the hip
Split the scene
You know the story
The crazy stand up wit
Poet-crazy-junkie high note
Mother-humping force of hurricane
Ripping away the billboards of life
Revealing the sad shallow underneath

You know this guy
Crucified with a shot of smack

And tabloid headlines
Tailored to the story
But the story was more than the story
It was an ellipsis
Three dots at the end
Interrupted thought
Dot . . . dot . . . dot . . .

Another Voice Speaking

Somewhere between night's chaos
And dawn's bitter glow
Your fingertips fold hours into minutes
And a man waits at the end of a street
For something, someone

Somewhere a voice calls
An echo of another time—a land
Cupped in a sound that lingers
At the edge of consciousness,
Somnambulistic
—a name without a name—
something in the air
a clock ticking backwards
towards the sea
a moment when life sleeps
and death opens a door through a wall
we never suspect is waiting for us

City Scapes

They look like maple leaves
But they're glass shards
Frozen on the sidewalk

El Mundo al Revés

It's a strange world we're living here
Where fat buzzards perch on trees
And good fruit lies on the ground
And all around children in their bare feet
It's a strange world we're living here

It's a strange mood on this block
Everywhere there's heavily armed cops
and a body or two on the street
that never had a chance to scream—Stop.
It's a strange mood on this block

Pues es el mundo al revés . . .
Donde van corriendo los pez
Y los pajaritos nadan
Y los gatos pardos ladran
Porque es el mundo al revés

It's a strange crowd in this classroom
The teachers prophets of death and doom
And the books with empty pages
And you win by hook or crook
It's a strange crowd in this classroom

It's a strange scene on this street
Where you learn to die or cheat
And it doesn't matter who you are

You're just another piece of meat
Because it's a strange scene on this street

It's a strange world they're selling here
Where no one looks you in the eye
And the budget goes for hate and war and fear
So the best thing is not to buy—anything
Because it is a strange world they're selling here

Es el mundo al revés
Donde van corriendo los pez
Y los pajaritos nadan
Y los gatos pardos ladran
Así el mundo al revés

Brujería for a Bad Check

On Friday dumb waiter
You'll feel the first runs
The mouse in your stomach
I grew there when I discovered
you'd given me a bum check
charged a bunch of drinks and desserts
ran a caballito, as we say in my
part of La Mission

So I've returned the favor
I've dropped lizards, frogs and a
spider or two in your soup

The sangría you serve tonight
will turn jaundiced
and your carefully placed napkins
will blow away

On Saturday things will change
the pots will revolt
and the spatulas will slap you around
you'll wind up pumping gas
wishing you'd never messed
with a poet

Shadows in the Mirror

Across Texas desert you carried
Ingots of sweat, and your family
Through New Mexican winters, & Arizona
Gila monsters and saguaro
Sons like adobe
Rooms filled with wine, grown from
Sand, heat, and the alluvial seasons
That formed traces on your face
Recalling arroyos where you raised
Yourself in the burnt air mountains
Of Chihuahua, in the mythic past of Tarahumara
Clouds and caravans for cities of gold
You step
Behind me in the mirror as I
Comb my hair today abuelo Agustín
Planting your tomatoes, the
Vines twining towards the sky
The heat of Logan Heights
Shining on your earthy hands
Your face cousin to Geronimo
Your hawk eyes
Your voice soft, your hands hard
It was another time, a world before
Mine, I didn't know your cups
Lined with rosy wine, didn't know
The places in your heart where
Thorns sprouted sweet as bell peppers

You grew, didn't know your wife,
Mythic-sized Ramona, who stepped
On thorns, who swept salt from the corredores,
Who sowed furrows while she waited, angry with
Rosettes of pain, hung like lanterns in
The windows of her eyes. The time
You burned down railroad car house,
Drunk asleep while the frijoles boiled, then
Homeless with seven—one my mother,
Other uncles lost in war, lost in auto
Factories, lost in the shadows of your bouts
With alcohol the opponent, the ring your living room
The decision: your sons absent from the
Picture above fireplace mantel.
I cannot recover the image, lost,
Cracked, abandoned. My
Eyelids, my hair, the pigment of my skin—
You stand behind me a shadow
In the mirror. I stand before you,
Grandson from another language,
Son of your dead daughter, Soledad.
Remember me? I am the line
Circling the desert, the miles of railroad
Bones tracing ourselves backwards
And forwards, spinning days out of
Golden air in Califas. I forgive you
The pain spread like petals. You
Wanted something, you willed
Me something from a hundred villages

In the Chihuahua mountains,
From a hundred sunsets patinated
On your face.
                In the silver mirror
You carried out of the desert
On the crushed hope of your shoulders
I touch your face, your eyes
And listen to you, and we
Speak of bones and blood,
                Even beyond the desert
                Beyond the hieroglyphs of death.

La Violencia de las Horas

Se siente en el aire
No se sabe de dónde vendrá
No se sabe ni dónde
Un tocón en la puerta
Una sirena de emergencia
Que viene por vos
O un balazo por la ventana
En la noche o al mediodía
Sin noticia avanzada
Ni mensaje text
Ni correo electrónico
Dará el aviso
Sentando en la silla de tu escritorio
O mirando televisión
Allí está—siempre al hombro
No hay protección contra esta violencia
Es el martillo de los locos
Al abrir la puerta de tu hogar
La bala perdida con tu domicilio
Que ya viene con tu nombre firmado
Y uno sigue viviendo con los ojos abiertos
Aguantando todo
Esperando el golpe

Black Mezcal

Sun-scorched streets of Oaxaca
black mezcal blindness
desperate bus ride through
isthmus of Tehuantepec
riding from town to town
ghostly deserted plazas
with indian names dark
as my face
forgotten bus stations
lights burning all night
forlorn end of the road
in a sad dead end town
sick with fever
mixing pills and cheap mezcal
jukebox cantina wailing
"San Marqueña de mi vida,
San Marqueña de mi amor . . ."
A red-eyed cantinero pierced hearts
with maguey needle
and the blood flows clear
on the sawdust floor

19 Men

19 men
slipping through the border
19 men
hiding in a railroad yard
19 men
trying to get a tough job
19 men heard a coyote howl
19 men with nothing to lose
       stepped into a Missouri-Pacific
              aluminum freight car
                     and the doors were sealed

19 men
going for a hard ride
19 men
riding through El Paso
19 men
sweating in the West Texas heat
19 men
and they won't get far
       without air to breathe

(Where's the light in this rolling coffin?
Let's strike a match,
let's see your faces—
There's el indio Jacinto & Isidro & his
compadre Jorge and los cuatitos Mingo & Monchi from
    Aguascalientes

who haven't eaten all day & there's Adrián the redhead
& Carlos el albañil & el zarco Tomás—
& Francisco who just got married, Pablo
who's never been kissed and that other Pablo too
& tall Gerardo y Felipe con su lápiz de estudiante
David who dreamt of his house, with his son David jr, barely
    fifteen,
Quincho el Nicoya
Memo el poeta & Mario who said
this was his last time & you Miguel Rodríguez)

19 men
riding in a death train
19 men
fighting off a bad dream
19 men
without air or water
19 men
who'll hear their screams
     crazy with heat convulsions
19 men
tore their hair ripped their skin
     smeared their blood
         on the refrigerated nightmare

19 men
     only one survived

19 men

Incantation for the Resurrection of Dawn in Haiti

Con tambor y maraca
Ayiti—place of mountains
Arawak-Mandinga-Ibo-Dahomé
Spirit of Toussaint
Spirit of Jacques Roumain
Spirit of Wailing Woman
Spirit of the People
Step forward in thunder & rumba

Spit out the demons—
Drum beat heart of mountain
Drum beat heart of river
Spit out the demons of poverty
Spit out that evil rot of debt &
Criminal banks that cannibalize
Your very children
Baraaph

Cha-cha and drum:
Ayiti place of mountains
O Creole Sondé miroir
Step forward Mistress Erzulie
Spread your wings like love
Step forward Ogún-Changó
Bring darkness to its knees,
Despair & madness

Will crash against your lightning bolt
Step forward Baron Samedi
Voudou the hell out of them bone suckers
Mount their vampire lairs
Their corporate boardrooms
Confuse their invasions at the crossroads
Let the zombies knaw
At their fingernails
And make them dance the dance of humanity

Rattle:
There is thunder. There is lightning.
Heralds of the new dawn
Where the Rada and the Petro work together
When workers earn a living wage
And farmers don't go hungry
And children have good schools with solid roofs
And hospitals are everywhere and they are free

Ayiti—place where mountains tremble
Where the sun squeezes through the gloom &
Dust of history
Beating heart of life
Beating heart of dawn
Hell yes dawn—sunrise, alba, sol, solazo

FIRE WATER EARTH SKY

Ayibobo! Ayibobo!
Ayiti—Place of Mountains
Ayibobo.

> Ayibobo Haiti reading
> February 28, 2010
> Glide Memorial Church

Homage for the Cockroach Poet

—for raúlrsalinas

Fire up that ball of Nepalese temple hash

Let the jazz flow under the porkpie hats
Let the zoots swing their high notes
Let the vatos float their lowrides
Let the rukas sigh their sighs
Let the conch shells blow hard and mighty
The Cockroach Anthem for the Cockroach Poet

And gather all los más chingones y chingonas
Los más danzantes los más guerreros
Las más valientes y los más poetas
A cantar himnos de lucha y justicia
Carve them in our own stone calendars
Our historic years, our heroes, heroines
Poets, warriors
This is we who were
Here's how we fought with pen in hand
(sometimes otherwise)

So let the sacred smoke flow
Let's beat the ancient drums
Let's sing the holy songs of struggle
Let's raise our clenched fist in last salute
Corazón en lucha
Bright this dawning in the east

Side of Austin, in San Antos, in Los,
La Mission, in Sacra, La Loma
all live etched eternally in your
epic howl/ llanto/ dream travel/ trip
to recover the barrio
that is all the barrios of the universe

And now the drum beat of the poet
Starts Life moving again

In this barrio and the next forever firme
Hail! The Cockroach Poet—y qué?

c/s

"Parker's Mood"

Jazz club, Naha, Okinawa
For raúlrsalinas

Sax man's
wild riffs
feel like home
to wayfarer lost in
alleys and backstreets
of Naha

"Nights in Tunisia"
in my rum
guitarist strums
where is home
old sailor
where the pillow
with strange dreams
I'm Mexican Ulises
washed upon
foreign shores
messages reach me via transpacific
meta-telepathic wave
lengths and they wail them solid beats
of poets long gone like jazz greats
Parker, Coltrane, Miles
here in groovy club where island
spirits mix with Chicano alma
that knows the rhythm of this or that

clipped to stirring neon red & yellow
glowing in Naha alleys where rum
spills from my cup
and I toast this coast
joined to hip of this other shore
blue in the notes strung
in the smoke of this jazzy
          jazzy
                    hip along
strip of melancholy
          who knows what.

Haiku

Before the vast open universe
Human scale only in a poem

Main Bar—Higashiyama

Last night in Kyoto
Cigars and rum
Satchmo wailing "La Vie en Rose"
Memories dissolve like ice
Tomorrow a shinkansen
For somewhere else
Or to nowhere

Caracas Is Not Paris

Caracas is nothing like Paris you said. As if any place could be like Caracas. César Vallejo had also lived in Paris and had died in that massive city of alleys and rancid puddles of human piss stinking up the subways. Vallejo had written about his Paris in *Poemas Humanos*, my own copy worn at the spine. And now here was the book again, resting on your lap, as you paused to smoke a cigarette, with the ennui of a chanteuse. The café in the Latin Quarter was filled with students, most of them exiles from places like Chile and Argentina and every other country of Latin America. Yours was Venezuela, but more than that it was Caracas. Like a caress in the humid Caribbean night scented with plumerias and menaced with billy clubs—that was your Caracas you said.

Later that night the band kept playing a vallenato "Gavilán Pollero" and wine and smoke and friends and nostalgia for somewhere else, which is the purpose of Paris, the essence of that city. To feel exiled, to live exiled. Until you read Vallejo's poem I did not understand the word. It was the dead of night, the candles out, you were on the bed, staring at the ceiling, when you recited "Piedra Negra Sobre una Piedra Blanca."

In Barcelona years later I would recall you for no reason when I heard the stories of the executions on Montjuic during the Spanish Civil War. At the end of that night in the club, as the band put away their instruments you fell into my arms sweet as a mango in the mercado. With the others watching I circled your waist while you smiled and it seemed to me a unique occurrence, Haley's comet prophesying the fall of Napoleon.

Vallejo died during the Spanish Civil War you said in the Louvre while you showed me the dead statues when all I really wanted was to look at you. As if Paris existed as a backdrop to your walk, sashaying across the boulevards, a red scarf around your neck, your hair in braids. You were more than anyone could ask for in one lifetime. Your voice, your words still echo in my own exile, without country or flag.

I did not believe you— believe what you said when you said you believed in the way you believed. But you meant what you said and I hope you never forgive me for doubting you.

You talked of streets that swallowed children, where rivers of sewage ran between the rows of houses and in those black waters mosquitoes thrived like flowers. And in the barrios children died daily for lack of aspirins or clean water. And right next to the most wretched hovels on earth rise magnificent palaces of marble and exotic woods where lords peer over the chaos like gods from the heaven. A city of skyscrapers and nightmares.

Guajira where you grandmother came from. Walked twenty-two days with four kids and no money to reach Caracas. But you were raised in the rich part of town and now in Paris on a scholarship you wanted to meet someone different, someone exotic and how much more exotic can you get than a Chicano in Paris. You said.

You would recite Vallejo's poem in the dirty rain of Paris as we sloshed our way through the Latin Quarter, one thousand years of urine staining the pavement, and the poster of

Rimbaud upon which I too left my yellow trail at the feet of the queer poet. Cars rumbling somewhere, a bus honking, children shouting in the apartments, our shoes squeaking on the wet cobblestones, and above it all your voice. Your haunting voice—*Me moriré en París con aguacero.*

My copy of *Poemas Humanos* so read and re-read and yet not a place mark on it, not a dog-eared page, not one fold or wrinkle on it, but worn down at the spine from the many times it has been cracked open in Paris, Mexico City, Los Angeles, San Francisco, the pages yellowed, frail and brittle like our lives.

I remember your body on the narrow bed, the areolas of your breasts, your hair spread on the pillow, the sense of being alive—young, in Paris, sipping coffee at a sidewalk café. But you would have none of it, the harsh cigarette and your black coffee. Your tiny grotto sparse as a nun's cell.

In a field beyond the soccer stadium dogs scavenged human bones and human fingers. You had worked with the forensic students exhuming the bodies. Whose bodies I asked. All our bodies you said. Our bodies so fragile like the dawn breaking over the llano and the parrots fleeing the first rumblings of the big cats, the jaguars, the panthers, their yawns like cannons' roar, echoes of ten thousand years ago, still alive. The song "Gavilán Pollero"—thirty years later I can still hear it—*Gavilán, gavilán, gavilán. Te llevaste mi pollera gavilán.*

Caracas grew old and withered because you were not there.

Paris was beautiful not because it was Paris but because you were there. And Paris without you would have been dead as all the dead soldiers of World War I, when people in the City of Light died of disease and famine and those that survived ate rats. And every animal in the zoo was eaten, including the ostrich, the red foxes, the white rhinoceros, all the monkeys, and the lions. The citizens of Paris spared nothing to stay alive. It was scorched earth all the way. The Army sweeping the llanos of campesinos, like the Parisians had swept clean the zoo. You couldn't stay there in Venezuela, even though you and your country had the same name. You couldn't stay here either—a bourgie med student on the Champs-Élysées where your less than ice-pale skin made you stand out, and children on the street pointed to your black hair in braids.

"*Me moriré en París y no me corro*"—Walter dead now, floating like Shelly in the waters of Venice—LA that is—poet wanderer to the end, his copy of *Poemas Humanos* on my desk and your memory with it.

Those nights in Paris spent in your studio, somewhere I don't remember, but do remember you, the shape of your waist, the mint taste of your mouth, your dream of Caracas like blue phantoms on the wall. You dreamt of children without hunger or tapeworms, of water without deadly amoebas, a world simple and clean for the children.

And you knew your dream was as wild and desperate as Vallejo's dream of a free Spain in 1938 when the Fascists crossed the Río Ebro and everyone knew all was lost.

The Orinoco runs through your life like a savage rain carving the land. One afternoon in the city where I live the Spanish-language television said you were killed in a shootout. You had an alias but I recognized your description. I turned off the television, the rest didn't matter. It wasn't in Paris where you died, it wasn't even on a Thursday.

It was Caracas—so many years ago, so many. But I still remember how you read that night in your grotto by candle-light, by cigarette smoke, your voice filled with blood and sweat and crimes and murders and redemption of a whole continent, and finally the words you knew so well—because they were Vallejo's, but also because they were yours too. And now Vallejo's poems linked forever to you and to Paris. *Poemas Humanos* yours forever in life and death and Caracas. Every-where lovers dream of a better world you will be there, you and Vallejo.

—*Tal vez un jueves, como es hoy de otoño.*

ACKNOWLEDGMENTS

The following poems first appeared in slightly different versions in these publications:

"Caracas Is Not Paris" in *Tri-Quarterly Review*, Northwestern University, 2013

"Cuatro Copas," "Report from Hell's Living Room," "Mission Vision," "Aquí con tu Memoria,""Brujería for a Bad Check," "Shadows in the Mirror," "La Violencia de las Horas," and "Homage for the Cockroach Poet" first appeared in *Native Tongue*, CC.Marimbo Press, Berkeley, CA, 2013

"Ahora Fuego/ Fire Now" in *Revolutionary Poets Brigade* Vol. 1, San Francisco, CA, 2010

"El Sueño de Lorca/ Lorca's Dream" in *Left Curve* No. 17, Oakland, CA, Spring 2010

"Tango Roto" in *San Francisco Bay Guardian*, June 1993

"Havana by Night" as a broadside, Sore Dove Press, San Francisco, CA, Spring 2000

"The Poet Recalls His First Reading," "Big Girls Don't Cry," and "Detalles" in *The Homestead Review*, Hartnell College, Salinas, CA, Spring/Summer 2001

"16th & Valencia" in *New Mission News*, San Francisco, CA, January 2000

"El Arete," "Three Seeds for Your Birthday," "The Eyes of the Poet," "The Beers, the Cigarettes, the Trash," "There's No Santos on My Altar" in *Spare Poems*, Luna's Press, San Francisco, CA, 2001

"Persuasion/ All the Reasons Why" in *Oxygen Magazine*, San Francisco, CA, 1993

The author would like to thank the following people for their support during the period that these poems were written:
Jack Hirschman and Agneta Falk—for insisting; Sal Garcia, David Volpendesta, Byron Spooner and Judith Ayn Bernhard, Jorge Argueta and Luna's Press, Ámbar Past in Chiapas, L's Caffé on 24th Street, Jack Boulware and Litquake, Randy at CC. Marimbo Press, and all those who gave me a chance to read and perform these poems. Of course, none of this would have happened without Magaly and Marisol watching over my shoulders.

Mil gracias . . . muy agradecido.